THE LIFE OF
THOMAS HARDY

THE LIFE OF
THOMAS HARDY

ANNA WINCHCOMBE

DORSET BOOKS

First published in 1978
Second edition by Dorset Books 1989

Copyright © Dorset Books 1989

ISBN: 1 871164 06 0

British Library Cataloguing-in-Publication Data
Winchcombe, Anna
    Thomas Hardy.
    1. Fiction in English. Hardy, Thomas, 1840–1928.
    Biographies
    I. Title
    823'.8

Printed and bound in Great Britain by
Penwell Print Limited

DORSET BOOKS

An imprint of Wheaton Publishers Ltd, a member of Maxwell Pergamon Publishing Corporation plc

Wheaton Publishers Ltd
Hennock Road, Marsh Barton, Exeter, Devon EX2 8RP
Tel: 0392 74121; Telex 42749 (WHEATN G)

SALES

Direct sales enquiries to Dorset Books at the address above.

PREFACE TO THE SECOND EDITION

This short study of Thomas Hardy's life, was originally published as *Thomas Hardy — A Wayfarer* to commemorate the fiftieth anniversary of his death. Now, 150 years after Hardy's birth, it is appropriate that this valuable work should again be made available to the public.
The author's intention is that the book should be of use to students of Hardy and his writings, but it will be of equal value to anyone who wishes to acquaint themselves with the background of Dorset's first man of letters.

Anna Winchcombe lived for thirteen years at Hardy's birthplace, Higher Bockhampton, and was commissioned to write this work by the Thomas Hardy Society and Dorset County Library Service.

ILLUSTRATIONS

CONTENTS

Page

1 · THE EARLY YEARS

Thomas Hardy was born on June 2nd 1840, in an isolated thatched cottage on a heath.
His people were builders and stonemasons and had built the house in 1800 at Bockhampton,
three miles from the county town of Dorchester, in Dorset. The child was thought to be
dead at birth and was thrown aside while the doctor attended to the mother, but luckily
the nurse saw that he was breathing and his life was saved. After this hazardous start he
was a delicate baby and little is recorded of him at first, save for the one strange story of
his mother coming in from the garden one hot afternoon and finding him asleep in his
cradle with a large snake curled upon his chest.

With care he soon grew into a lively child who could read early and loved music so much
that he was moved to tears when his father played popular tunes on his fiddle, and would
dance madly to hide the fact that he was weeping. His closest companion was his sister
Mary, born nearly two years after him, and later two more children, Henry and Kate, completed the family. Mary Hardy, his grandmother, stayed with them until her death and she
was a link with the past for the boy, who loved to hear her stories of old customs and super-
stitions, and of events that took place long before his birth. In a poem that he wrote about
her - *One We Knew* - she appears

> **With cap-framed face and long gaze into the embers -**
> **We seated around her knees -**
> **She would dwell on such dead themes, not as one who remembers,**
> **But rather as one who sees.**
>
> **She seemed one left behind of a band gone distant**
> **So far that no tongue could hail:**
> **Past things retold were to her as things existent,**
> **Things present but as a tale.**

The boy's mother, Jemima, was a small, lively woman of strong character and talented in
many ways, good at needlework and an excellent cook. She read quite widely and encouraged her eldest child to read also. He remembered her going about her housework cheer-
fully, singing romantic songs, and walking with him on the heath, along the white path that
was once a Roman road, picking bunches of heather and fern and finding flint knives and
arrow-heads that even earlier inhabitants than the Romans had left there.

Hardy's father was a fine-looking man, tallish, very straight-backed, with a bearded face,
white and regular teeth and clear blue eyes that never faded. He had courteous manners
and this helped him in his business dealings with the county ladies, but he was not really a
tradesman at heart and could never be persuaded to leave his rural surroundings and set up
a more prosperous concern in the town. His chief passion was music, and he played his
fiddle at the local dances and also in one of the little orchestras of violins, 'cellos and clari-
nets which provided the music in the village churches before the organ was introduced. As
a boy, Hardy enjoyed attending church and listening to the hymns. On wet Sundays, when
he was not allowed to go there, he would drape himself in a white tablecloth and recite the
Morning Service to a congregation of two, his cousin and his grandmother.

The family in their lonely home lived very close to Nature. As he woke in the morning Thomas listened to the sparrows coming down their long holes in the thatch to the open air, and he could recognise the different bird songs in the dawn chorus in the garden. On the heath he watched the deer and the foxes and rabbits, and learnt the habits of the smaller creatures too, the snakes, lizards and gnats. His sense of hearing was so acute that he could distinguish between the sounds the various kinds of trees made when the wind blew through them and could hear the distinctive whisper of the dried heather bells. He was always curious and perceptive. When he was quite young he knelt down one day in a field of sheep and pretended to eat grass, just to see what the sheep would do, and found when he looked up that they had gathered in a circle round him and were regarding him with great surprise. His tenderness towards the less fortunate of human beings, which is such an important element in his writing, started with a sensitivity to the suffering of animals. From a journey he made with his mother to London at the age of eight or nine, he brought back as one of his main memories the cries of the ill-treated animals in Smithfield Market. To the end of his days he remembered the feeling in his hands of the half-starved body of a fieldfare that his father had accidentally killed with a stone one bitter winter's day.

The people he observed as a boy in his home were later to become the characters in his novels; his family and his near neighbours in the hamlet of Bockhampton, the men who came regularly to the house to practise hymns and carols and to eat and drink at the Hardys' expense, friends invited to dances, funerals and christening parties. The boy listened to the gossip and the story-telling and the country humour and almost unconsciously absorbed the material for his writings about these people and their joys and tragedies.

There was plenty of sadness in the lives of the men and women of his native county in the period when he was growing up. The Hardy family at Bockhampton became quite comfortably off over the years, but many of their relatives were in very poor circumstances and several of them emigrated to the colonies to find a better life. There was malnutrition and disease in the overcrowded cottages of the Dorset agricultural labourers and little security in their work. The men who came to be known as the Tolpuddle Martyrs, who lived only a few miles from Hardy's home, tried to found the first Trade Union to help their fellow workers and were deported to Australia for swearing an illegal oath. Riots occurred frequently and were savagely broken up.

It was not until the Education Act of 1870 that state schools began to be built in England, but Hardy's parents decided in 1848, when Thomas was eight years old, that he was strong enough to start his schooling. He was naturally a shy, reserved boy and felt unwilling to make any changes in his quiet life. Much later, he wrote a poem about his attitude at this time to growing up, *Childhood Among the Ferns,* in which he pictures himself lying on a rainy day in the shelter of a house of ferns.

> **The sun then burst, and brought forth a sweet breath**
> **From the limp ferns as they dried underneath:**
> **I said: 'I could live on here thus till death;'**
>
> **And queried in the green rays as I sate:**
> **'Why should I have to grow to man's estate,**
> **And this afar-noised World perambulate?'**

Thomas Hardy, senior

Jemima Hardy, Thomas Hardy's mother

In his story of his life he also describes himself at this age, lying on his back in the sun and looking at the rays coming through the gaps in his old straw hat, thinking how useless he was and how he did not want to grow up. "He did not want at all to be a man, or to possess things, but to remain as he was, in the same spot, and to know no more people than he already knew (about half a dozen)." When he told his mother about his lack of ambition she was very much hurt. In his last novel, *Jude the Obscure,* the reactions of the hero as a boy to the threat of the outside, adult world are similar to Hardy's own, and his fear of becoming a man even greater. Yet Hardy did emerge from his sheltered home bravely enough. He went first to the village school in Lower Bockhampton, a mile from his own hamlet. This had been built for Mrs Julia Martin, the lady of the manor of Kingston Maurward, where Hardy's father did the estate work. It was intended for the children of Stinsford parish who had only a temporary building nearby. Mrs Martin took a great interest in Thomas and he had a warm affection for her. He was the first pupil in the new school and waited nervously that morning for the others to enter two by two with their teachers. He showed himself to be a bright pupil and was particularly good at reading, arithmetic and geography. At home he was encouraged as usual by his mother who gave him books to read, among them a translation of the Greek poem, *The Iliad.* His interest in history was stimulated when he found some old numbers of a magazine his grandfather had left in a cupboard, called *A History of the Wars,* and in those torn pages he read stories about the battles of Napoleon, illustrated with crude pictures of soldiers and their weapons and the dead bodies on the fields.

After he had been a year at Lower Bockhampton his ambitious mother, feeling that her son should have a better education, sent him to Mr Last's Nonconformist school in Dorchester, even though the Hardys were Church of England people. This move offended Mrs Martin and meant less work for Hardy's father on her estate and a break in her warm friendship with the boy. Later she was to forgive him and greet him kindly when they met once at a harvest dance, but he was not to see her again until he was quite grown up. Hardy described his school days in the autobiographical *Life,* which he prepared over the years and left for his second wife to edit and publish after his death. He was a bright pupil who "galloped unconcernedly over the ordinary school lessons" and he started to learn Latin at the age of twelve and later won a prize in this language. He also studied French and German, and read Shakespeare's plays, he admitted, for the plots only and did not think highly of *Hamlet.* He was taught drawing and mathematics and was especially interested in algebra, finding "a certain poetry in the rule for the extraction of the cube-root, owing to its rhythm". In all, he received a good education for a country boy of those days and one that lasted until he was 16 years old.

He studied well at home and rose regularly at 5 am to read at his window in the bedroom he shared with his young brother. Then he went down the ladder staircase to the warm kitchen beneath to get his breakfast and started off on the three-mile walk to Dorchester, first by the lane then over the fields to Stinsford church and on by the water meadows to Greys Bridge at the entrance to the town. At the end of the day he came back by the same route, sometimes with school friends with whom he was popular. Even at this age, however, he liked best to be alone, to walk by the clear waters of the River Frome or to linger in the churchyard, reading the names on the old gravestones and thinking about the lives of those buried beneath them. He always tried to avoid being touched by his fellow pupils and this peculiarity remained with him all his life, so that he disliked "even the most friendly hand being laid on his arm or his shoulder".

His solitary nature did not prevent him from going out in the evenings, all the same, whenever the opportunity arose, to play his fiddle at dances in the neighbouring farmhouses. He was such an enthusiastic musician that on one occasion he went on for three-quarters of an hour without a break, until the hostess stopped him in case he should burst a blood-vessel. Sometimes his father went with him and they would return together in the early hours of the morning, seeing strange sights in the dark lanes, like the white, headless figure propped in the hedge which turned out to be a drunk man in a smock, whose head had drooped on his chest. Mrs Hardy did not disapprove of these outings but she did insist that Thomas must not take payment for his playing. Only once did he accept a few shillings for his services and with this he bought a copy of *The Boys' Own Book* which remained in his library ever afterwards.

The boy was growing up. When he left school he began to help his father in the business, but a local architect soon noticed the promising lad among the workmen and, having tested him, offered him an apprenticeship at a reduced premium. His parents were very pleased and paid the whole premium at once and Thomas started on his training. He had thought himself a bookworm and at one time imagined that he might enter the Church, but he meekly fell in with his parents' plan for him and entered the office of John Hicks in Dorchester. He found his employer to be a kindly man and his fellow pupil, named Bastow, was a lively colleague with whom he joked and argued and read books, not only on architecture but the classics and poetry as well. Hardy went on with his private studies and began learning Greek, doing most of this work between 4 and 8 am, at his bedroom window as usual, before getting ready for his walk to the town. Next door to the office was a school run by a man who had a great influence on him, William Barnes, the Dorset poet and scholar, and to him he would run for a decision on some point of argument or an interpretation of a poem.

It was a good life for the young man, with plenty of activity and companionship. There is a photograph of him at this time, showing a youth dressed in a shabby coat, a large black hat under his arm and a look of determination in the eyes and mouth. He was popular with many different kinds of people and would still rush off in the evenings after work, usually with his father and uncle, to weddings and christening parties and Christmas celebrations at some remote house. Father and son played the violin and the uncle the 'cello, a country pop-group of the day, and they were much in demand since they still charged nothing for their playing and were most energetic performers. A description of such an occasion comes as early as his second published novel, *Under the Greenwood Tree,* and is a witty account of the kind of dance he must often have attended. There are such scenes in most of Hardy's novels and the dance seems for him to have a symbolic meaning, relating to the development of the plot and to the ever-changing attitudes of the characters towards each other. Hardy was by now a much stronger young man than his early life had promised, and, as he says in his autobiography, he managed "like a conjuror at a fair, to keep in the air the three balls of architecture, scholarship, and dance-fiddling, without ill effects".

His attitude to women at this time was one of distant admiration and he lost his heart several times to girls who were almost complete strangers to him. A gamekeeper's daughter with beautiful red hair; Louisa, a farmer's daughter to whom he never said more than "Good evening"; a girl on a visit from Windsor - all these he idealised and even wrote poems about them long afterwards. Other contacts he had with local girls at the Sunday School where he taught along with two sons of the Fordington vicar, the Revd Henry Moule. Here he met dairymaids and servant girls who would sometimes ask him to write their love letters as they were not good at expressing themselves and he learnt in this way at second-hand some of the mysteries of the human heart.

Horace Moule was his special friend at this time and with him he would walk in the fields around the town, talking about books and writing. Hardy had begun to compose poetry himself, mostly short verses on simple subjects. The first known poem is one called *Domicilium* -

the youth was showing off his knowledge by using the Latin word for "home" - and it describes the cottage at Bockhampton and the life his grandparents lived there when they first came to the district. For a boy of sixteen it is a most promising effort, factual and romantic, but as yet Wordsworthian rather than Hardyean in tone. He also tried short articles and humorous verse, some of which appeared in the local paper. His more serious poems of this date were not published until much later, since editors, used to a more conventional type of poetry, were puzzled by his realistic style.

The town of Dorchester he immortalised in the novel, *The Mayor of Casterbridge,* which deals with life in the middle of the century. It was in many ways a violent time and he describes all aspects of life there, from the noble to the sordid. In one of his short stories, *A Changed Man,* he tells of the cholera epidemic that swept through the district, when the Revd Henry Moule supervised the burning of the victims' clothes in the fields below the town. Another story, *The Withered Arm,* centres round the old belief that a deformity could be caused by witchcraft and cured by touching the neck of a newly-hanged man. Public hanging was still a form of entertainment in Hardy's young days and there were savage penalties for minor crimes. Hardy records in the *Life* that he was sitting at his breakfast in the cottage one morning when he remembered that a man was due to be hanged at 8 o'clock at Dorchester. He took up the big brass telescope that had been handed down in the family and hurried up to the spot on the heath from which he could see the town. The sun was shining straight on to the white front of the gaol and the executioner and the officials could be seen in their dark clothes, but the crowd below was invisible at the distance of three miles. Just as he placed the glass to his eye the white figure of the victim dropped downwards and the faint note of the clock struck eight. The whole thing had been so sudden that the glass nearly fell from his hands and he "seemed alone on the heath with the hanged man, and crept homeward wishing he had not been so curious". This was the second and the last public execution he saw, the first having been a year or two earlier when he stood quite close to the gallows and saw Martha Brown hanged. She was a woman who had murdered her husband in a fit of jealous rage and for once Hardy's sensitivity seems to be lacking in his later description of the scene, for he remarks how well her body looked in its gown, silhouetted against the sky, as it swung round from left to right.

At the age of twenty-one Hardy had serious thoughts of becoming a Greek scholar and perhaps entering a university, but the prudent Horace Moule advised him against this and urged him to continue with his architectural training so that he could fulfil his parents' hopes for him and begin to earn some money by the time he was twenty-two. Hardy realised that this was sensible advice - he was always very meek about obeying people he admired - and he gave up the study of Greek from that moment and began to think of getting a job. He turned his attention to London as a place of employment. Could he have been slightly influenced in this choice by a senior pupil named Fippard at Hicks' office, who used to come back from trips to the capital talking of the dance rooms in the great city? He would speak of the Cremorne and the Argyle and hop round the office floor with an imaginary partner in his arms, humming the tune of a quadrille that haunted Hardy for many years and to which he could never put a name. Whatever the attraction might have been for this young man in the West Country, he did, on Thursday April 17th 1862 (he records the exact date in the *Life)* set off alone for London, with a return train ticket in his pocket for safety's sake, which he threw away after six months.

8

2 · LONDON LIFE

It was a rather immature Thomas Hardy who arrived in town and presented letters of introduction from Dorset friends to two architects there. The first was most polite and did nothing for him. The second sent him to a Mr Arthur Blomfield, at whose drawing office he began work as assistant almost at once. This office was soon moved to 8 Adelphi Terrace and from the window, on a clear day, there was a beautiful view right along the Thames with its many bridges. When the weather was bad and everything seemed to be the colour of brown paper or pea soup it was not quite so pleasing.

Many years later Hardy wrote of the sensations of a young man from Dorset, plunged into the life of the capital, wandering through the maze of the city streets, with few friends and exposed to many temptations. He seemed to lead an active life at first; visited galleries and coffee-houses, saw Kean act Shakespeare at Drury Lane, attended the Opera at Covent Garden, heard Charles Dickens at one of his popular readings. He went to the Cremorne and Argyle dance-halls that he had heard about, sophisticated and even notorious haunts that the more disreputable elements of society frequented, and searched in vain for the quadrille tune that the architect's pupil had taught him. He also bought himself an old fiddle and played on it in his lodgings at night, with a friend to accompany him on the piano, and in the daytime at the office his employer and the pupils would sing part-songs.

His mother in Bockhampton must often have been anxious about him in his new life and he kept in touch constantly by letter with his family and with his sister, Mary, training to be a teacher in the college in Salisbury. Remembering an old friendship, he called one day on Mrs Martin, the lady of Kingston Maurward manor, who was now living in London. The visit was not a success, for the young man of twenty-two was very different from the child she had befriended and she had also greatly altered in her looks. They wrote to each other often after this meeting but he never saw her again.

He went on with his reading and writing as a relief from office work and composed many poems which he sent to various editors. He had such a respect for their judgement at that time that, when they rejected his manuscripts, he scarcely ever sent the poems to another paper. It was sometimes thirty or forty years later, when he was famous as a novelist, that these early compositions saw the light of day. He did publish at this time, however, a humorous article called *How I Built Myself a House,* which appeared in *Chambers' Journal* in 1865, and it may have been this minor achievement which encouraged him to try his hand at writing prose.

About this time he had one of those fits of depression which recurred at intervals during most of his life and he wrote in his diary: " June 2nd. My 25th birthday. Not very cheerful. Feel as if I had lived a long time and done very little. Walked about by moonlight in the evening. Wondered what woman, if any, I should be thinking about in five years' time." It was one of these moods that inspired the bitter poem, *Hap,* where he rages against the blindness of Fate:

> —Crass Casualty obstructs the sun and rain,
> And dicing Time for gladness casts a moan ....
> These purblind Doomsters had as readily strown
> Blisses about my pilgrimage as pain.

One rather odd experience that he had was not likely to make him more cheerful and was typical of the strange things that happened to the young Hardy. It was the period of the expansion of the railways and cuttings were being made through the city itself, for trains to pass to the stations. Sometimes they went across churchyards and Blomfield was asked to supervise some of these diggings to see that the human bones were properly removed to other burial places, and not taken off to bone factories. When the Midland Railway wanted to cut their line through Old St Pancras Churchyard he asked Hardy to supervise the clerk-of-works and to go in unexpectedly in the evenings and other times, to see that all was well. The young man watched the coffins being dug up and new coffins being provided to replace those that came apart when lifted, and he would listen to the gruesome conversation of the workers. A high fence had been placed round the churchyard and flares were lit in the evenings. Preoccupation with death was a characteristic of Victorian writers and Hardy was no exception in this, for many of his poems deal with burials and graveyards and there are several scenes connected with gravediggers and corpses in his novels. He certainly had some first-hand experience of such matters in his vigil at St Pancras and was even able to see a comic side to the affair for he tells us in the *Life* that once when Blomfield himself looked in on the churchyard a coffin was opened to reveal a skeleton with two skulls. Years later, when the architect met Hardy after a long separation his first words were: "Do you remember how we found the man with two heads at St Pancras?"

Under the strain of city life Hardy's health began to deteriorate and by 1867 he became so weak he could scarcely hold the pencil and set square for his drawing. He blamed this partly on his habit of reading from six to midnight after work and also on the living conditions in general and the evil smells from the river in particular, the city's drainage system not having been constructed then. There were psychological reasons for his breakdown as well, for the countryman had been exposed to new influences in the city and had lost his faith in the traditional beliefs of his forbears. As a result of reading the works of men like Huxley, John Stuart Mill and Darwin, Hardy became an agnostic but remained emotionally attracted to the church and its rituals, and he experienced the tension that existed between the old life and the new. This tension created drama in his life and in his writings.

When he visited Dorset his friends were shocked by the change from the healthy young man they had known to the pale, city man he had become. He longed to return to his native county and, when his old employer, John Hicks, wrote asking him to recommend someone to work with him on church restoration, he said he would go himself and left London late in July 1867. Back at his home in Bockhampton he began to recover his strength, and after a few weeks in that peaceful atmosphere he was quite healthy again, and walked in and out to Dorchester each day as of old, falling into the routine easily and helped by an ability to tackle practical problems as a result of his experiences in London. He found time, too, to turn to his writings again and began a novel which he called *The Poor Man and the Lady*. He had taken the first step towards literary fame.

a   *The old school, Stinsford*

b   *Bockhampton Bridge from the river path*

3 Thomas Hardy aged nineteen

2 The window in Hardy's bedroom at the cottage

It was a hard road at first. In July, 1868, he sent off his finished book to Macmillans, the publishers, and had a quick reply from the head of the firm, Alexander Macmillan, who told him he had read it with interest and that his writer friend, John Morley, had admired parts of it but thought other scenes were too fanciful, "so that they read like a clever lad's dream". Hardy was given the manuscript back and was half pleased that two such important people had paid his work such close attention. During the autumn he rewrote some of the pages and in December was given an interview with Mr Macmillan, who told him that his firm could not publish it but gave him a letter to Frederick Chapman, head of Chapman and Hall. Hardy called at the office with his manuscript under his arm and this visit, though rather unsatisfactory at the time, led to another meeting early in 1869, when Chapman offered to publish the book if Hardy would agree to guarantee £20 against loss. Hardy said he would do this and went home to wait for the proofs to arrive. Instead of receiving them he had another summons to London, where the famous author, George Meredith, who had read the manuscript for Chapmans, now advised the young man not to let this rather too radical and realistic work go to the printer, even though the offer still held. "The critics would be about his ears like hornets", Meredith believed, and his future career would be injured. He told Hardy to rewrite the story, softening it down greatly, or to put it away and try his hand at a purely artistic novel with a strong plot.

Hardy made a few more attempts to get the book into print, then gave up the battle and later wrote most of it into his first three published novels. A large part also appeared in a novelette called *An Indiscretion in the Life of an Heiress,* published in the *New Quarterly Magazine* in 1878. It is a simple love story with a few signs of the radicalism of which he was accused.

Architecture was still his profession and although John Hicks died at this time Hardy worked on some unfinished church restoration for the man who took over the business, Mr Crickmay. After this was done he was taken on for a three-month period at Crickmay's Weymouth office, and was glad to feel that he had at least that amount of secure employment before him.

He was now twenty-nine and still boyish enough to enjoy the life of the pleasant seaside town. He went out boating and swimming in the beautiful bay every summer evening, listened to the town band playing Strauss waltzes, danced in a hall where they taught the quadrille and where "a good deal of flirtation went on". In this cheerful atmosphere he began another novel, trying to follow Meredith's advice to leave out social satire and elaborate his plot. He called it *Desperate Remedies.* Once more his days were filled with work, writing and the dance.

When he wanted to concentrate on his book he went back to his home at Bockhampton, and he had nearly finished it in February 1870 when Crickmay wrote asking him to go to Cornwall to take particulars of a church he was intending to rebuild there.

Crickmay's words: "Can you go into Cornwall for me?" were the prelude to a series of events that were to change Hardy's life. He had felt a little unwilling to undertake the journey but agreed to do so, since he had only a few chapters of his book to finish and he was interested in church restoration. He was also keen to see the county of Cornwall, which he associated with the legend of King Arthur and thought of under its romantic name of Lyonnesse.

He records that on March 7th 1870 he rose from his bed at 4 am, had his breakfast, and went out into the frosty garden, with the stars still shining in the dark sky. Down the lane he had so often walked to school and work he went, his sketch book and measuring tape under his arm, an unfinished poem in his pocket. He caught the early train to Yeovil and waited two long, cold hours there for his connection to Launceston, where he arrived at four in the afternoon, and hired a horse and cart to take him to St Juliot, the parish where he was expected. It had been a fine day with a dry breeze but it was cloudy and quite dark by the time he had been driven the sixteen miles to the rectory. The vicar, the Revd Caddell Holder, was in bed with a sudden attack of gout and his wife was looking after him when Hardy arrived at the front door. The only person left to receive him was a lively young woman with a fine complexion, steady grey eyes, a good figure and a lot of light brown hair done in ringlets. This was the vicar's sister-in-law, Emma Lavinia Gifford, and she was a little shy at having to greet the bearded stranger, with his soft voice and a slightly different accent from those to which she was accustomed. She thought him at first sight much older than he really was, and very business-like, but she was puzzled by a blue paper sticking out of his rather shabby greatcoat and was surprised when he later told her this was a poem he was writing and not a plan of the church he was to inspect.

Hardy made drawings of the aisle and tower that were to be rebuilt and stayed rather longer than he had meant to do on this first visit. He came back often, while the restoration was going on, living at the rectory and roaming the sea-coast with Emma, she in a brown habit riding on her brown mare, he walking by her side. They had picnics in the romantic Valency Valley that led from her home to the town of Boscastle and they sketched on the cliff tops, with the sea stretching before them and the sea birds flying round them. At night the family gathered, as was the Victorian custom, in the rectory sitting room and listened to the two sisters singing duets. Once they all drove in a trap to Tintagel and Hardy and Emma climbed to Arthur's castle and stayed too long there and were shut in and waved their handkerchiefs from the top to summon rescuers. In these new and strange surroundings, among people with a different background to his own, Hardy fell in love.

He and Emma were both nearly thirty years old and had had other attachments before they met. Hardy was practically engaged to his cousin Tryphena Sparks, a dark-haired beauty who lived near his home. But they parted soon after he met Emma and he was from then on faithful to his new love. In his third novel, *A Pair of Blue Eyes,* he describes the Cornish scene, and the portrait of the heroine, Elfride, is a close enough likeness of Emma herself as she was when he first knew her, charming, light-hearted and impulsive. The poem, *When I Set Out for Lyonnesse,* also captures the magic of that time.

When Hardy went back to work after this first meeting he wrote many times to "the young lady in brown" and posted books to her and told her of the progress of his novel. He sent *Desperate Remedies* to Macmillans when it was finished but they again refused his work and he realised that it was because they did not like sensational novels like this one, which was a kind of early crime story with an involved plot and some weird incidents. For a second choice he tried a publisher called Tinsley who made an offer to publish the book on certain terms. Hardy returned to Cornwall in August to find the young lady in brown changed into a young lady in blue, which suited her far better, and this visit was a very happy one. The round of picnics and walks began again. The old church tower, the reason for his first journey, soon came down and Hardy regretted its destruction for he had begun to see that much damage might be done in the name of restoration.

Back in London, Hardy sent Emma some of the chapters of *Desperate Remedies* to be copied, the original having been rather damaged. Tinsley had asked for £75 in advance from the author and poor Hardy, with only £123 in the world and practically engaged to a girl with no money, agreed to this and the book finally appeared anonymously, as was often the custom in those days, and in three volumes, in March 1871. At last the young man found himself in print and the novel luckily had two good reviews, one in the *Athenaeum* and the other in the *Morning Post.*

That good luck did not last. Down in Dorset again, Hardy walked out from the town towards his home on the morning of April 22nd, with a copy of the *Spectator* under his arm, sat down on a stile and read a cruel review which stated that it was just as well that the author of *Desperate Remedies* had not used his name as it would have been disgraced for ever. It was "a desperate remedy for an emaciated purse" joked the reviewer, which was none the less wounding for being quite true. Horace Moule read the review and wrote to Hardy telling him not to mind it too much, but he never forgot the words he had read that day on his way home to Bockhampton, when he wished that he were dead.

The *Saturday Review* followed later with a good notice that "brought the volumes back to life" so he recovered a little and even, in his amiable way, admitted to himself that the *Spectator* might have been right to some extent. He started, with his usual determination, on another novel, this time using an uncomplicated plot and setting the story in the house and village where he was brought up and filling the stage with the friends of his boyhood. It was to be called *Under the Greenwood Tree* and was a simple love story that followed the seasons of the year, with a sub-plot about the church choir and orchestra. There was some social comment, too, and shrewd observation of character, especially in the case of the flirtatious, enigmatic heroine, who might well have been based on his cousin Tryphena. In this work Hardy first began to create a West Country world of his own, which he later called by the old Saxon name of Wessex, with the local towns and villages disguised under names like Mellstock, Casterbridge, Budmouth and so on.

He wrote the novel in his parents' home, and had only to look out of the window to see the scenes he was describing. He remembered that the critics had said that the rural passages were the best in his first, rejected book, and he concentrated on this type of life now, writing in a relaxed and happy mood, in spite of previous disappointments. He sent the manuscript off to Macmillans once more, and this time they liked the work and would have been willing to publish it later on, even if they did not think it would have a very general appeal; but Hardy, over-sensitive about rejections and criticisms, told them to return it at once and threw it into a box along with his poems. It was a disheartening ending to a hopeful project, and an ironic stage in Hardy's relationship with the firm of Macmillan, who were later to become his sole publishers and to rank him as their best-selling author.

Both Emma and Horace Moule advised Hardy not to despair and to stick to his writing, but he turned to London and to architecture once more and felt that a literary career was too hazardous, especially as he had received the statement of the *Desperate Remedies* account and found that he had only £60 back from the £75 he had paid as guarantee. His publisher, Tinsley, met him in the street one day, however, and asked if he had anything more written and Hardy said he might be able to retrieve the manuscript of a novel he had thrown aside. His parents found the book in the cottage and he sent it to Tinsley without looking at it and with no interest in the matter. He was offered £30 for the copyright and this he accepted, and later £10 was added when the book appeared in a foreign edition. With this modest sum he was in print once more. *Under the Greenwood Tree* appeared anonymously in June 1872.

This time the *Spectator* commended the book and other reviews were kindly and appreciative, so that Tinsley was induced to ask the author if he would write a serial for his magazine. Hardy agreed to do so, on somewhat better terms, and immediately felt that he had been rather rash since he had not got another novel ready and, what was more, had never written a serial in his life. He asked for a month's holiday from the office where he was then working and went home to his lodgings in Westbourne Park and started on *A Pair of Blue Eyes,* the novel with the Cornish setting. Once more he had to retire to Bockhampton to finish it. It came out as a serial in *Tinsley's Magazine* at the end of the year and was published in book form in May 1873. Hardy was relieved to find that the *Spectator* again gave him a good review.

Later that year, when he had begun to write another novel in the seclusion of the family home, he received the tragic news of the suicide of his friend, Horace Moule, in Cambridge. He deeply regretted that the two people who had been such a strong influence on his career, his best friend and the woman he was going to marry, had never met each other. Meantime, his romance was progressing well. The couple paid visits to London, Bath and Bristol, and to Tintern Abbey on the Wye, where they recited some of Wordsworth's lines on that great ruin. At the age of thirty-three he had fairly started on his literary career and had achieved this by a strong determination and a belief in himself, helped not a little by good advice from his friends and by a certain amount of luck.

Emma Lavinia Gifford, Hardy's first wife

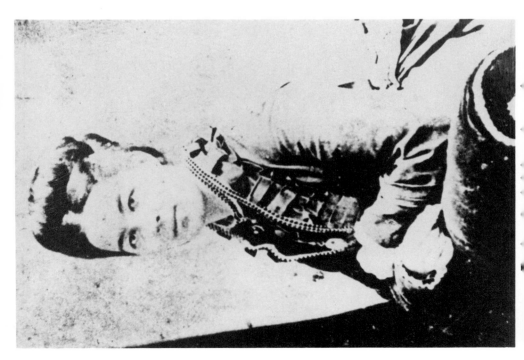

Kate Hardy as a young woman

a Stinsford - footpath to the river

b Stinsford Church

5 · RECOGNITION AND MARRIAGE

The new novel was *Far from the Madding Crowd* and was the first to bring him general approval and fame. It came out as a serial in the *Cornhill Magazine,* edited by Leslie Stephen, a great critic and writer of his day who had liked Hardy's work and had written asking him for something for his paper. Here again luck played a part, for this letter was given to some children to deliver to the cottage and was dropped in the mud, from which a labourer rescued it.

In the autumn of 1873 Hardy was writing this new work, once more against time, sometimes up on his bedroom window-seat, sometimes on the heath, scribbling notes on large dead leaves and wood chips or on pieces of stone or slate left lying there, preferring these unconventional materials to a pocket-book, which always "made his mind as barren as the Sahara". This time also he was within walking distance of the main scene of his story, for the village of Weatherbury in the book is based on Puddletown and the heroine's farm was the large manor called Waterston House, over the ridge from the cottage. This nearness he found inspiring, as usual.

At the start of 1874 the first instalment appeared, after a few arguments with Stephen about certain passages the editor thought should be omitted because the magazine public might consider them improper, although to modern readers the book can be considered to have a high moral tone. Hardy wanted to make sure that the illustrations would show the rustics to be intelligent people as he had described them and not the boorish types other writers of Victorian fiction were apt to portray. He was anxious, too, that the farm implements, costumes and buildings should be authentic and sent one or two sketches as models. He heard no more from the publishers and was surprised and delighted when he opened a copy of the *Cornhill Magazine* that he had bought in Plymouth station, on the way back from a Christmas visit to Cornwall, and found his story at the beginning of the magazine, with striking illustrations by a woman artist, Helen Paterson. He sent off a copy to Emma at once and she was pleased to learn that she had been right to encourage him to continue with his writing.

It was still an anonymous work and readers began to try to guess the name of the author. It was suggested that it might be George Eliot, and this annoyed Hardy, for although he thought her one of the greatest living authors he felt that she did not have a real understanding of country people. A friend of Hardy's was pestered by those wanting to find out the name and sex of the writer and she would reply: "*It* lives in the country, and I could not very well introduce you to *it* in Town". Hardy's circle of friends and acquaintances did noticeably increase at this time, however, and he paid many visits to London.

In July 1874, all the story was finished, the last chapters being written "at a gallop". The pages were posted off to Stephen and in September Thomas and Emma were married in St Peter's Church in Paddington, the ceremony being performed by Emma's uncle Dr Gifford, Canon of Worcester. Years later Hardy discovered his wife's description of that day in a secret diary. She wrote: "The day we were married was a perfect September day ..... not brilliant sunshine, but wearing a soft, sunny luminousness; just as it should be." After a short visit to the Continent the couple settled in Surbiton. *Far from the Madding Crowd* was published in book form in November, by the firm of Smith, Elder.

It was typical of Hardy's modest attitude to his work that he did not realise at first how much interest his latest book was creating, but at last he and Emma did notice that a great many people, and women especially, were carrying a copy around with them. The critics were mostly kind. The *Spectator* admitted that there was "a new light among novelists", although other papers found it less good and some called it inartistic and unconvincing. But Hardy was becoming a little better at ignoring these judgements and stated that he just hoped to be "a good hand at a serial" so that he could make enough money to live on, since he had practically given up the profession of architecture by this time.

This story of a woman farmer and her lovers is not just a good serial but one of Hardy's masterpieces, in which he creates a convincing world of his own and characters of universal interest. The hero, Gabriel Oak, is no conventional rustic but a real and complicated man, and Bathsheba, the heroine, develops from a rather flighty young girl to a mature woman who learns the truth about love through suffering. Hardy is already an expert in the art of novel-writing, using the agricultural theme, with its descriptions of the lambing, sheep-shearing and harvest as a frame for the human story of passion and cruel deception and violence, ending with the promise of married bliss. Hardy must have felt glad that this solid success came at the start of his own marriage.

His relationship with Emma was at first a happy one. They moved to rooms off Westbourne Grove in 1875, along with their few belongings at that time, all in four fairly small packing cases, two of which and part of a third were filled with books. They went to theatres, museums, concerts and parties. Hardy had begun a novel with scenes of London life and once more he wanted to be in the place he was describing. He knew that his readers preferred him now to write about country people and to stick to his sheep and his shepherds, but he set his new novel in town society, with the result that not only his public but he himself began to feel that his writing was becoming a mere trade and not a product of inspiration and emotion. *The Hand of Ethelberta* seemed immature and lifeless after the powerful appeal of *Far from the Madding Crowd*. Some critics praised it when it came out in book form in 1876, but most readers received it coldly and found the situations impossible. Once more he was told not to take too much notice of criticism. Leslie Stephen, who had become a close friend, wrote to him: "You ... have a perfectly fresh and original vein, and I think the less you bother yourself about critical canons the less chance there is of your becoming self-conscious and cramped." This was sound advice to Hardy from one who was a critic himself, but to the end of his writing life he was still capable of being hurt by adverse notices in the Press and opposition from certain sections of the public.

Self-conscious and cramped was scarcely the tone of the next novel, *The Return of the Native,* in which the action is once more in the district around his home and the actors based on people well known to him. It was written in the Dorset village of Sturminster Newton, where Emma and Hardy settled after short stays in the seaside town of Swanage and in Yeovil in Somerset. This moving from one house to another in the early days of their marriage shocked their relatives who accused them of "wandering about like two tramps", but now, in the summer of 1876, they took a two-year lease of a house above the

River Stour and there spent the happiest of their days together. They had no furniture as yet so they bought £100 worth of mid-Victorian things in two hours in Bristol and made Riverside Villa a pleasant place to live in. They enjoyed village life, took part in local events, and rowed on the River Stour in the summer evenings among the water-lilies, while workers in the fields waved to them and swallows flew out of the bushes.

In the *Life* Hardy notes that they found their young servant with her lover in the early hours of one morning and dismissed her, an action that seemed to him regrettable. When they heard later that she was to have a baby he adds sadly: "Yet never a sign of one is there for us". Another entry at this time is interesting with regard to Hardy's attitude to descriptions of Nature, which feature so greatly in his works. "September 28: An object or mark raised or made by man on a scene is worth ten times any such formed by unconscious Nature. Hence clouds, mists, and mountains are unimportant beside the wear on a threshold, or the print of a hand."

The Return of the Native appeared as a serial in the magazine *Belgravia* during 1878, and was published in book form at the end of that year by Smith, Elder. Although this novel now ranks high among his works, neither the critics nor the public were very enthusiastic about it at first. *The Times* remarked that "the reader found himself taken farther from the madding crowd than ever" and perhaps the remote lives of the heath dwellers and the tragic fate of the heroine, Eustacia, and of her husband, Clym Yeobright, half-blind and reduced to near poverty, were not so readily appreciated as the intrigues of happier rustics or the doings of the farming community.

When Hardy was revising the novel at the age of seventy-two for the Wessex Edition of his books he found Clym to be the nicest of his heroes, though not a bit like himself. But there *is* a resemblance between Hardy and this kindly and serious man who comes back, after a period of town life and culture, to his native heath where he had played as a boy with the flint tools he had found there among the heather and the yellow furze, his friends the snakes and wild ponies and the human beings who haunted that barren stretch of country.

By the time the Sturminster Newton period was ending Hardy's career was progressing well and publishers were anxious to have his prose writings, even though his poetry was still unknown. But there were signs that his marriage was not set on the same successful course. Later he wrote a poem, *A Two-Years' Idyll*, about these early years with Emma and asked:

> What seems it now?
> Lost: such beginning was all;
> Nothing came after: romance straight forsook
> Quickly somehow
> Life when we sped from our nook,
> Primed for new scenes with designs smart and tall ....
> — A preface without any book,
> A trumpet uplipped, but no call;
> That seems it now.

Early in 1878 the Hardys left Dorset for London, "primed for new scenes", and took a house in Trinity Road, Tooting. Hardy seemed to think that he should be in touch with the literary life of the capital. A garden party at the Macmillans, a studio meeting with the son of the poet Shelley, dinner with Matthew Arnold and Henry James, lunch with Tennyson - all these events must have made him feel he was in the heart of things again. He records many parties in his diaries, one of which he describes wittily - a Soirée Musicale at a literary club: "A large gathering. The whole thing a free and easy mix-up. I was a total stranger to everyone else: sometimes two or three of these total strangers would fraternise from very despair".

In the winter weather he was apt to become very depressed and noted once in his diary for a November morning: "Awake before it was light. Felt that I had not enough staying power to hold my own in the world." One bitter cold February day he paid a visit to his family in Dorset, being met at the station by his brother Henry, now a builder like his father. Going on horse and cart through the sleet to Bockhampton, the east wind cut into him like a knife and, in the light of the lamp at the end of the town, he could see Henry's hand glistening with ice. Yet he enjoyed his visit and picked up a few stories of the old days from his father and went to Weymouth and Portland while he was there. He valued his roots and his memories of the past. One day in Tooting he heard an organ-grinder playing the tune the architect's apprentice had danced to in the Dorchester office and he ran out hatless into the street and pursued the young foreigner in the hope of learning the name of the dance at last. "Quad-ree-ya!" was all the man could say, showing him the list of tune titles in front of the organ, and "Quadrille" was all that it was called. Hardy never did find the real name nor did he ever hear the tune again.

Did Hardy really like town life? He says of himself in the *Life:* "To go about to dinners and clubs and crushes as a business was not much to his mind. Yet that was necessary meat and drink to the popular author. Not that he was unsociable, but events and long habit had accustomed him to solitary living." The city atmosphere still oppressed him. In his diary for the dawn of May 19th 1880 he noted that he could not sleep that night for he had the strange feeling that he was lying "close to a monster whose body had four million heads and eight million eyes". Under these conditions, however, he had managed to write another novel to please his publishers and some poetry to please himself. The new book was *The Trumpet-Major,* a historical work about the threat of the Napoleonic invasion of England, made lively by the use of tales told to him by old people who were young at the time.

a Cornhill, Dorchester, c1900

b South Street, Dorchester, c1900

6 - TO DORSET AGAIN

The Hardys visited Cambridge in October 1880 and stayed a week, seeing the sights and attending the 5 o'clock service at King's Chapel, where Hardy fancied he saw Wordsworth's ghost wandering among the fan-traceried vaulting in the roof. Hardy was feeling like a ghost himself, physically very weary, and this was a sign of the start of a long illness which developed as soon as he returned to Tooting. He was bleeding internally and the Macmillans' doctor, who had been sent to examine him, gave him the alternative of a dangerous operation or a treatment that involved months of lying in bed. Hardy chose the latter and was nearly six months in this state, being cared for by Emma and dictating his next novel to her. *A Laodicean* had already begun to appear in *Harper's Magazine* and it had to continue somehow, partly for the publisher's sake and also for the interests of his wife, for whom he felt he had as yet made poor provision should he die. It is not surprising that this story is a weak one, probably the least interesting of all his works. The strain of his illness and the need to have Emma standing between him and his inspiration were the reasons for the dullness of the story, though the hero as architect should have been a compelling subject for Hardy.

While Hardy lay in bed all through that winter he made notes on many things; the deaths of great writers like George Eliot and Thomas Carlyle, and the statesman, Disraeli; vague thoughts on politics; the germ of the idea for a great Napoleonic Ballad; the movement of the snowflakes outside the window; and more domestic matters, like boots becoming mildewed through lack of use, clothes old-fashioned, umbrella rusty, and children seen from his window growing taller.

In June 1881 he recovered enough to make the journey to Dorset again, to a house in the town of Wimborne, and to a garden full of old-fashioned flowers and ripening fruit. He corrected the proofs of *A Laodicean* here for publication in book form, sitting under a great vine through whose leaves the sun tried to shine, throwing a green light on the paper. *Two on a Tower,* the story of the tragic love affair of a young astronomer and the lady of the manor, was written here, and his social life blossomed again, with local play-readings, trips to London and to Scotland, and a ball at the house of Lord and Lady Wimborne. He was also writing short stories, among them one for children, *Our Exploits at West Poley,* a caving tale with a moral twist.

After two more years at Wimborne the Hardys moved to Dorchester, at first to yet another furnished house near the top of the town. At last the "two tramps" were to be settled people, however, for Hardy had bought a plot of land one mile east of Dorchester and Henry had begun to build to his brother's design the big redbrick house that was to be called Max Gate, and would be their home for the rest of their lives. Hardy planted trees in his new property on New Year's Eve, 1883, and he and Emma browsed over the Roman remains discovered when the hole for the well and the clearing for the foundations of the house were being dug, showing that others had long ago lived and died on that spot. The house took eighteen months to build and at last, in June 1885, the two slept there for the first time.

R L Stevenson called on them soon after they had moved in, the first of many famous men to visit Max Gate. He did not know Hardy personally until then but he admired his work greatly. Hardy had written *The Mayor of Casterbridge* while waiting for his new home to be finished and early in 1886 it began to appear in the *Graphic* magazine and in *Harper's Weekly*. "I fear it will not be as good as I meant," he commented in his diary, thinking that it had been spoilt by being in serial form, but this re-creation of the Dorchester of his boyhood, with its powerful story of the rise and fall of the tragic hero, Michael Henchard, shows no sign of lack of continuity, and was as popular as his other major novels with the reading public; and even Hardy later admitted that the plot was "quite coherent and organic, in spite of its complication". It was published in book form in May of that year.

According to the novel, the Dorchester of around 1850 was a grim place but to the resident of Max Gate at the end of the century it was a county town he enjoyed living in. He remained at heart the simple man, participating in the life around him. One New Year's Eve he joined the bell-ringers in St Peter's belfry and admired the energy with which they rang out the Old Year, the red and white ropes they held "bolting up through the holes like rats between the huge beams overhead". He went to every circus that came to Fordington Field, watched the strolling players acting Shakespeare's *Othello* with amateurish gusto on their stage in the market place, noted how four shabby girl musicians, playing in the High Street on a cold winter's day were transformed by the light from the shop windows at night to creatures of "wondrous charm" and wrote a poem about them, *Music in a Snowy Street:*

> **The weather is sharp,**
> **But the girls are unmoved:**
> **One wakes from a harp,**
> **The next from a viol,**
> **A strain that I loved**
> **When life was no trial.**

Life should not have been a trial in the great new house but there was already tension there between the husband and wife and an increasing difference in their attitudes to such matters as morality and religion. Emma was becoming more eccentric with the years and Hardy himself was not an easy man to live with, absorbed as he was in his work and shunning too personal human contact. Outwardly, their social life continued energetically, with frequent visits to London and to aristocratic country homes, but Hardy always seemed to return with relief to what his friend Lady Portsmouth called his "benighted Dorset", to his house and garden where the pines, beeches and sycamores that he had planted were gradually becoming taller and finally formed a thick screen that hid the building and its occupants from the road so that they seemed to be living "at the bottom of a dark well of trees". The ferns of his childhood were larger now and he could retire from the world under them and write the stories that were to bring him world-wide fame and compose the poems that placed him in the front rank of English poets at last.

Hardy used three different rooms as a study in Max Gate, the first being just above the drawing room, where he began to write in 1885 *The Woodlanders,* his own favourite "as a story". In October of that year his old friend, William Barnes, died in his nearby rectory and Hardy walked over his favourite field path to Came Church for the funeral. As he went he caught a gleam from the sun's rays reflected on the coffin being carried along a lower road, and commemorated this in his poem *The Last Signal,* describing how

> **Thus a farewell to me he signalled on his grave-way,**
> **As with a wave of his hand.**

The Woodlanders started to appear as a serial in May 1886, and in book form it was published by Macmillan in March 1887. The *Spectator* paid it a mixed compliment, saying that it was "a very powerful book, and as disagreeable as it is powerful", but the rural people and the descriptions of the wooded country where they lived had their usual admirers. The scene is set in North Dorset but the feeling of the woods is so clearly conveyed that it seems likely that he was thinking of the plantation beside his Bockhampton home, where he would still wander, recording on one birthday visit that he saw strange faces and figures formed by the dying light, leaves shining like human eyes and the patches of sky between the tree trunks looking like ghosts and "cloven tongues". This description he repeated later in the novel.

Just the day before the publication of *The Woodlanders* Hardy and Emma were off to Italy. He was an ardent frequenter of the haunts of the famous, finding it inspiring to watch the sunset from the very bridge where Shelley must have stood, picturing Keats dying in the house on the Spanish Steps in Rome; more strangely, noting a similarity in Byron's Venice between the sound of the bells of San Marco and the "tin-tray timbre" of the church bells in his home villages.

There is a description of Hardy at this time of his life which he quotes as if he approved of it: "His smile was of exceptional sweetness, and his eyes were a clear blue-grey. His whole aspect was almost childlike in its sincerity and simplicity, the features being strongly marked, and his nose, as he himself once described it, more Roman than aquiline. The nobility of his brow was striking. When young he had abundant hair of a deep chestnut colour, which later became a dark brown, almost black, until it turned grey." Well-shaped hands, neat shoulders, and a light, quick walk complete this rather flattering picture, with the added comment that he was a slim man but would never allow himself to be weighed as he considered it unlucky. Later, perhaps because of his prominent nose, Charles Morgan called him "a small bird with a great head", and John Cowper Powys likened him to a falcon. Leonard Woolf wrote of his charm and apparent simplicity, which hid the fire within.

In August 1889, Hardy settled down daily to write his new novel, one as yet unnamed that was to be his greatest and for which he already had three requests from magazine editors eager for a new serial from his pen. When, however, the early chapters were offered to these editors, they refused them on the grounds that it was an improper story. The author then began the task of taking out those parts of the novel that might be considered shocking to the magazine reader of the day. This was very dreary work and was done, as Hardy says, in a spirit of cynical amusement. That he undertook it at all shows again that amiability in Hardy's nature, some might even call it cowardice, which made him fall in with the wishes of others. The revision was finished late in the following year and the story began to appear in the *Graphic.*

Tess of the d'Urbervilles, as the novel was finally called, was a powerful and moving work that roused great interest in the literary world. The bare outline of the plot sounds melo-dramatic enough; the tale of the country girl seduced by the son of her employer, giving birth to an illegitimate child that dies in infancy, marrying a pious young man who leaves her when he is told of her past, and finally murdering her lover when the husband returns to be reconciled with her. It is the way Hardy tells the story, his deep-rooted sympathy for his characters, his sensitive descriptions of the natural scene and the poetic beauty of his language that raises it far above other novels in the rural tradition.

The parts that the editors wished to be omitted were such incidents as Tess's christening of the baby on the night of its death, or the bodily lifting of the milkmaids over a flooded patch in the road by the hero, Angel Clare: in the magazine version he uses a wheelbarrow. In 1891, however, Hardy began to put back all the passages he had removed and the novel was published in November of that year by Osgood, McIlvaine in England and by Harpers in the United States in the following year. Luckily by then the International Copyright Act had been passed and it meant that Hardy had more profit from the sales of this novel than he had ever had from his other books.

It also brought him greater fame and a very mixed reception from the critics, some of whom thought it his most powerful book, another called it "a grim Christmas gift", while the *Saturday Review* said that the characters were "stagey and farcical" and that it was "an unpleasant story told in a very unpleasant way". Most of the objections were levelled against the sub-title of the book, *A Pure Woman,* since it was felt that such an adjective should not have been applied to a girl like Tess.

Readers' reactions were both rapturous and hostile. Controversy about the heroine arose in all classes of society. Farmers' wives in the West Country waited eagerly for their copies of the *Graphic* to come through the post and would waylay the postman with questions about Tess's fate. The Duchess of Abercorn, a society hostess, told Hardy that his novel saved her the trouble of sorting out her friends at dinner parties: if they thought Tess a "harlot" who fully deserved hanging she put them in one group, while those who referred to her as "poor wronged innocent" were invited on another evening. Women wrote to Hardy saying that their life stories were like that of his heroine and asking for his advice, but he did not feel capable of telling them how to run their lives and burnt all their letters. Meanwhile thousands of copies of the book were sold.

Hardy defended Tess to the last, and most readers today would agree with him as to her purity, with the reservation that she was perhaps a little too meek in her attitude to life. Here, more than in any of his other novels, Hardy seems to be saying that the odds were against anyone like Tess having a happy life, since all through the story there are accidents and coincidences that bring about her downfall, but to say flatly that Hardy was a fatalist, that his human beings are ruled by mere Chance, is to ignore the way in which character influences action in his stories. Chance plays a large part but it is not the only mover.

The value of the book as a piece of social history and as a criticism of the agricultural conditions of the day has been more appreciated by later readers in this century and Tess and her kind have been seen as victims of the laws governing life when there was a general decline in rural living standards. Hardy sympathises with their hardships and miseries and gives telling descriptions of the work in harsh fields and farms, but he can also convey the idyllic aspect of lives spent in happier surroundings, when Tess and Angel meet in the Valley of the Great Dairies, where the River Frome runs through the meadows.

Perhaps it was the extreme reactions to this novel that made Hardy comment that it was "the beginning of the end of his career as a novelist". The end came with his next novel, *Jude the Obscure,* which he began to write in 1892. It came out as a serial, once more expurgated, in *Harper's Magazine* in the United States in 1894 and 1895, and as a book, with the missing parts replaced, in England and America in November 1895, from the same publishers as *Tess of the d'Urbervilles.* The latter novel, meanwhile, was being translated into many European languages and was even serialised in a Moscow periodical, where it was read and approved of, according to Hardy, by the great Russian writer, Tolstoy.

In the years that he was making notes for *Jude* his life had followed the usual pattern, his trips to London being fairly regular, where he observed the people in the parties and meetings he attended with his usual detached and quizzical air, appreciating the writers and the duchesses he met, but noting also the girl who held a long-stemmed narcissus under his nose as they passed each other in the dark in Piccadilly. After returning from one of these visits he wrote: "Am glad I have got back from London and all those dinners: London, that *hot-plate* of humanity, on which we first sing, then simmer, then boil, then dry away to dust and ashes!" This was written in April 1892 and later in the summer of that year his father died at his cottage. Hardy had been paying almost daily visits to him in his illness and regretted that he had missed the very day he died. In recording his death he likens him to Horatio in *Hamlet:* "A man that fortune's buffets and rewards Hast ta'en with equal thanks".

A note he made in his diary about this time might well have been advice to himself as to how to react to the flood of criticism that came with the publication of *Jude the Obscure.* "Never retract", it went. "Never explain. Get it done and let them howl". Certainly they did howl and the first to make sounds of disapproval was Emma, who had grown so apart from her husband over the years that she now seemed to share little of his outlook on life. She thought the book too autobiographical, too revealing of Hardy's attitude to marriage, and called it "Jude the Obscene". She even went up to London to see an important writer of the day, Sir Richard Garnett, to ask him to stop the publication of the novel. Hardy himself considered that the story "would not bring a blush to a school-girl's cheek" and this is certainly the view that modern readers would take, but the critics and even the general public of the time saw it for the most part as a work of gloom, grime and indecency. The *Illustrated London News* stated that "the reader closes this book with a feeling that a huge pall has blotted out all the light of humanity". Another writer called the author "Hardy the Degenerate". The Bishop of Wakefield piously threw his copy into the fire and boasted of his action. Hardy was sceptical about this story, "knowing the difficulty of burning a thick book even in a good fire, and the infrequency of fires of any sort in summer", and his more serious reaction was to say that "the ethical teaching of the novel .... was as high as that of any of the bishop's sermons."

An American woman writer thought the book shocking - *"Tess of the d'Urbervilles* was bad enough, but that is milk for babes compared to this ...." she wrote. "When I finished the story I opened the windows and let in the fresh air." This critic, however, had the nerve to write to Hardy for an interview when she later came to England and he replied to her with dignity and, one feels, with not total honesty: "My respect for my own writings and reputation is so very slight that I care little about what happens to either, so that the rectification of judgements, etc., and the way in which my books are interpreted, do not much interest me." This was carrying his motto of "Let them howl" into practice, but it cannot be said that he was entirely deaf to the howling.

As a footnote to the Bishop's action Hardy's second wife quotes an extract from the magazine *Theology* in August 1928, where a Church of England minister advises priests about to become village rectors to read the works of Thomas Hardy, from which they could learn about "the essential dignity of country people and what deep and passionate interest belongs to every individual life". The ghost of Hardy can be imagined giving a very wry smile at this advice. In life he was amazed at the outcry against his novel and at its withdrawal from some of the lending libraries. Some people were even known to read it in brown paper covers, so as to hide the title. At least a few of the critics liked the book and realised that it was the most powerful and moving work that Hardy had produced. He himself described it as an attempt to show the contrast "between the ideal life a man wished to lead, and the squalid life he was forced to lead". Hardy put some of himself into the character of Jude Fawley, although he had made a success of his life where Jude was a failure, and there is very clear comment in the story on the problems of married life that he was facing with Emma. The heroine, Sue Bridehead, bears some resemblance to his friend, Florence Henniker, whom he had met in 1893 and with whom he had a close relationship based on the exchange of ideas similar to those held by Jude and Sue. It is the climax of his prose writing as well as the end of it and it might be regretted that Hardy did not go on to produce even more outspoken works in the present century.

It was partly the lack of understanding shown by the critics and by some of the readers - "A man must be a fool to deliberately stand up to be shot at" - but partly also a feeling that he had said all he wanted to say in this form, that made him give up novel writing. Another book, *The Well-Beloved,* was published after *Jude* but written before it, and it was a strange, symbolic story of a man pursuing his ideal love through three generations of women. This also received bad reviews that surprised and grieved Hardy. Short stories had appeared in magazines all through this period and were collected under the titles of *Wessex Tales, A Group of Noble Dames* and *Life's Little Ironies,* and the last volume, *A Changed Man,* was not published until 1913. But Hardy the novelist might be said to have died in 1895 and Hardy the poet began to take his place. While his outward life was pursuing its customary course of visits to London and the Continent, with the new excitement added of bicycle rides with Emma and Henry to places as distant from his home as Bath, Gloucester and Cheltenham, his thoughts were turning to the work he loved best and by which he most wanted to be remembered.

Max Gate

Florence Dugdale, Thomas Hardy's second wife, at Max Gate

At this time Hardy the dancing-man died also.   At an open-air event in Wiltshire, in September 1895, he introduced some country dances and hundreds of couples took part under the light of thousands of lamps and "the mellow radiance of the full moon".   But this left him stiff in the knees for several days and was probably the last time he ever trod a measure.

Hardy began to look out the old poems dating back to his early days and to write new ones, finding it difficult at first to express himself in verse but soon getting used to it. His first collection, *Wessex Poems,* was published in 1898 and received praise from the critics, mixed with surprise that a prose writer of such standing should turn to poetry at this late stage in his career. Hardy was strangely less moved by any criticism of his poetry than he had been by that levelled against his novels, for he admitted that he wrote his verses because he wanted to say the things contained in them and with no thought of pleasing anyone in his mind.

He knew that he struck a new note in poetry and that he had at first been misunderstood since his style was unlike that of the fashionable poets of his day, the late Victorians and even the Georgians. He had a very individual vocabulary and used uneven metres of great diversity and irregular rhymes, for he felt that he could express his thoughts better this way, believing that too regular a beat was bad art. He was beginning to be appreciated as a poet before his death, though to the end he still sent a stamped addressed envelope with his contributions to the papers so that they could be returned without trouble. There are now 947 poems in Hardy's *Complete Poems,* and these, along with fourteen novels, over forty short stories, two verse dramas and many articles make up a great output for any writer.

The 19th Century ended for Hardy with the writing of one of his best known and most moving poems, *The Darkling Thrush,* where he pictures himself listening to the song of the bird on a grey winter's evening, a song so ecstatic, he says

> **That I could think there trembled through**
> **His happy good-night air**
> **Some blessed Hope, whereof he knew**
> **And I was unaware.**

It was strange that this man, who had achieved so much success, should retire to his study and write novels and poems that were for the most part sad in tone, dealing with human tragedies in the tenderest terms and describing hopeless passions, betrayal, disillusionment and despair. Some of these things he had experienced himself but he was also capable of entering into the minds and hearts of others and revealing their thoughts and feelings as if they were his own. There are, of course, many comic scenes and characters in his novels and not all the poems are on sad themes. Some are lighthearted and witty, written in an almost conversational style. No subject is too great or too small for him. He can write of the sinking of the Titanic or of the Battle of Waterloo, then turn to the reactions of a wagtail drinking at a stream or mark the death of a favourite cat with the poem, *Last Words to a Dumb Friend:*

> **Pet was never mourned as you,**
> **Purrer of the spotless hue,**
> **Plumy tail, and wistful gaze ...**

Sometimes there is a whole short story in a few lines of verse, as in the poem, *At Tea,* where a couple entertain a guest, with very different reactions:

> **And the happy young housewife does not know**
> **That the woman beside him was first his choice,**
> **Till the fates ordained it could not be so ...**
> **Betraying nothing in look or voice**
> **The guest sits smiling and sips her tea,**
> **And he throws her a stray glance yearningly.**

Hardy's strength in his poetry, and in his prose work as well, lies in his direct personal appeal to the reader. He rarely indulges in sentimentality, does not rely on illusory comforts, comes to no smug conclusions about life and death. He wrote once that there was more autobiography in a hundred lines of his poetry than in all his novels and this does seem to be true.

While the private man worked hard in his study, the public man was leading the life of a well-known writer, visiting and entertaining busily. In May 1901, a literary club was invited to Max Gate and when Hardy's mother heard of this she insisted on her two daughters pushing her in a wheelchair to the main road, where the open carriages were due to pass on their way to Dorchester. The three women waited under the trees and Mrs Hardy waved triumphantly at her son's visitors when they appeared. They did not know until many years later that it was Hardy's mother who had greeted them by the wayside.

Three years later she died at Bockhampton. She was a woman whom Hardy described as one of dignity and judgement, who had been a great influence on him all his life. The poem, *After the Last Breath,* is a moving tribute from a son to his mother, where he expresses his relief that at last -- she was 91 when she died --

> **Our well-beloved is prisoner in the cell**
> **Of Time no more.**

Later the brothers and sisters put up a brass memorial to their parents in Stinsford Church, the words on it written in Latin, because Hardy believed that that language would remain more unchanged than English in the future.

In 1901 the next volume of poetry appeared, *Poems of the Past and the Present,* and the following year Hardy was working on *The Dynasts,* a play in verse about the wars of Napoleon which he had started some time before. In 1903 the first part of this long work was sent to Macmillans and other poems were published in papers and magazines. The publication of *The Dynasts* was completed in 1908. Two years later Hardy was awarded the Order of Merit in the Birthday Honours.

The parties at Max Gate became grander and more frequent in these years; on one occasion a marquee 150 feet long was put up in the garden for the entertainment of 200 journalists. The Hardys themselves attended a Royal garden party given by Edward VII at Windsor Castle in 1907. During seasons in London Hardy met Bernard Shaw, Maxim Gorky, H G Wells and Joseph Conrad. He mourned the death of Swinburne and Meredith in 1909, and at a performance of Milton's *Comus* at Cambridge he saw the young Rupert Brooke in the role of the attendant Spirit, and regretted that he did not speak to him then. *Tess* was performed as an opera in Covent Garden, but was so "Italianized" that Hardy scarcely recognised it as his story. *Far from the Madding Crowd* was produced in Dorchester and came off better, since he described it as a neat achievement. This year also the third volume of his poetry appeared, *Time's Laughingstocks*. New Year's Eve found him with a choking sore throat, which kept him in his room, crouching by the fire and hearing the "muffled peal down the chimney ... from the neighbouring church of St George".

In spite of minor irritations and illnesses, life seemed to be going well for Hardy and he must have felt more secure than ever before; but in the winter of 1912 Emma died suddenly, after a very short illness, and this affected him more deeply than he could have foreseen. She had complained of tiredness and heart trouble earlier that year and may have had some presentiment of her death, for he relates how she had sat down at the piano one day and begun to play all her favourite old tunes. Hardy went out while she was doing so and later wrote in the moving poem, *The Last Performance:*

> When I returned from the town at nightfall
> Notes continued to pour
> As when I had left two hours before:
> 'It's the very last time,' she said in closing;
> 'From now I play no more.'
>
> A few morns onward found her fading,
> And, as her life outflew,
> I thought of her playing her tunes right through;
> And I felt she had known of what was coming,
> And wondered how she knew.

Shortly after her death he found the little book which she had called *Some Recollections,* written some years earlier and describing their first meeting in Cornwall. On reading this he was filled with remorse that he had not attempted to bridge the gulf that had come between them and it was in this mood that he began to compose some of the finest love poems in the English language. Emma, distanced from him now in death and buried in Stinsford churchyard beside his parents' graves, roused more heartfelt emotion in him than she had done when alive. He wrote in the poem *The Going:*

> I seem but a dead man held on end
> To sink down soon ... O you could not know
> That such swift fleeing
> No soul foreseeing —
> Not even I — would undo me so!

On March 6th, forty-three years almost to the day since he had set out for Lyonnesse, he went back to St Juliot and walked along the cliff tops where he had courted the young lady in blue, thinking he heard her voice again.

> Can it be you that I hear? Let me view you, then,
> Standing as when I drew near to the town
> Where you would wait for me: yes, as I knew you then,
> Even to the original air-blue gown!

Or is it only the breeze, in its listlessness
Travelling across the wet mead to me here,
You being ever dissolved to wan wistlessness,
Heard no more again far or near?

This poem, *The Voice,* and others dated 1912-1913, he called under the collective title of *Veteris Vestigia Flammae,* "the remains of an old fire". Hardy was now at the height of his poetic powers and writing of his work at this time he quoted something that had been said of the poet Gray, but which was equally appropriate to himself, that he was "in flower" in these days and "his flower was sad-coloured".

After returning from Cornwall he set off in June to Cambridge, to receive the honorary degree of Litt.D. The man who, in the 1860s, had given up the idea of going to the university to get a pass-degree, was now being entertained by the Vice-Chancellor and many of the professors and receiving from them their greatest tribute to a man of genius.

For 14 months or so he lived alone in Max Gate, looked after by his servants and visited by his closest friends, but he now needed a more personal relationship and in February 1914 he married again, his bride this time being a woman much younger than himself, Florence Dugdale, who had been a friend of Emma's and had helped Hardy with his manuscripts. Life seemed to become more happy and secure but in the midst of a round of garden parties and lunches in the fine Dorset summer the First World War broke out and Hardy was right in thinking that it would last for years and bring great disaster in its wake, even though there were many who considered it would be over by Christmas.

Although he had written about wars and even conveyed some of the glamour connected with soldiers in battle in *The Dynasts* and elsewhere, he had long believed that common sense would prevent any further conflicts occurring between peoples on a large scale and he was now thrown into despair about the future of mankind, realising that he had not reckoned with the power still held by the governing castes in Europe, "whose interests were not of the people". In spite of his melancholy he entered into the war effort and joined a group of writers in London, where the streets were "hot and sad, and bustling with soldiers and recruits" and made plans to bring out poems and articles to assist the Allied cause. The man whose grandmother had been ironing "her best muslin gown" when the news came through that the King and Queen of France had been beheaded in the French Revolution now heard of the invasion of Belgium by the German forces. This war finally destroyed any hope Hardy had of the gradual betterment of mankind and any idea that there was "a fundamental wisdom at the back of things". The purblind Doomsters were in full command again.

In Dorset, Florence and Hardy helped at the soldiers' canteens, visited prisoner-of-war camps, arranged for some of the poetry manuscripts to be sold for Red Cross funds, and towards the end of the war sent the manuscript of *Far from the Madding Crowd* to be auctioned at Christie's in London for the same cause. On the day of the sale they both cycled up to Bockhampton and sat in the garden looking up at the window where the young man of thirty-four had written his early masterpiece.

His companion of the childhood days, his sister Mary, died in 1915 and was buried under the yew-tree where the other members of his family lay. Hardy remembered her with fondness and wrote of her mild and unassertive nature. In his poem written in December that year, *Logs on the Hearth, A Memory of a Sister,* he thought of the apple-tree they played in together:

> My fellow-climber rises dim
> From her chilly grave —
> Just as she was, her foot near mine on the bending limb,
> Laughing, her young brown hand awave.

At night he would lie in his room at Max Gate and think of those across the fields in Stinsford churchyard and of the many others dead on the battlefields. Although he was happy enough in his second marriage, he was still saddened by memories of his first wife and went on more pilgrimages to the scenes of his Cornish romance, taking Florence with him. She showed very admirable tact and consideration while he wandered round Boscastle and St Juliot, re-living his time there, or when he visited the house at Sturminster Newton which he had not entered for forty years and which roused sad reflections on the shortness of the happy period of his married life with Emma.

In the first year of the war a collection of poems, *Satires of Circumstance,* appeared. The Golden Treasury Edition of a selection of his poems came out in 1916 and another book of new poems was published in the following year under the title *Moments of Vision.* The poet was busy and so was the public man, championing many causes when the war was over - the prevention of cruelty to animals, always a matter near to his heart, the promotion of the idea of making Palestine a national home for the Jewish people, the project of establishing a South-Western University in Exeter. Between 1922 and 1925 two more volumes of poetry were published, *Late Lyrics and Human Shows,* as well as another verse drama, *The Queen of Cornwall.* The final book of poems, *Winter Words,* did not appear until after his death, and the last poem in that group is the one called *He Resolves to Say No More,* in which he asks:

> Why load men's minds with more to bear
> That bear already ails to spare?
> From now alway
> Till my last day
> What I discern I will not say.

Hardy in his last years was an enigmatic figure. Some who knew him spoke of his being withdrawn, melancholy, mean, a hermit in the well-protected house and garden of Max Gate. Others thought him benign and witty, fond of young company, with an intellect as clear as it had ever been. In his eighties he was certainly still bright-eyed and upright, enjoying his daily walks along the field-path to Came church with his unruly dog, who died two days after Christmas in 1926 and for whom there is a tombstone in the garden and a poem to his memory, *Dead 'Wessex' the Dog to the Household*. Almost to the end Hardy continued to write poems and to assemble details of his life story. He also wrote and received innumerable letters on all kinds of subjects. One from a friend asking him for his philosophy of life he answered rather deprecatingly: "I have no philosophy - merely what I have often explained to be only a confused heap of impressions, like those of a bewildered child at a conjuring show".

He still welcomed kindred spirits to his home, one of whom was T E Lawrence, who had a cottage a few miles from Dorchester and who would arrive in the drive "like a thunderbolt" on his large motor-cycle and go to sit by the fireside and to listen to the older man he so much admired. Walter de la Mare, J M Barrie, G B Shaw, Siegfried Sassoon, the Woolfs - these and many more came to see him at this time. Local actors performed scenes from *Tess* in his drawing-room, carol singers, like those in the old Mellstock choir in *Under the Greenwood Tree,* sang outside his window in the cold December air, players from Oxford acted Greek dramas on the lawn in summer-time and Hardy talked with them and admired their "boyish ardour and their modesty". He had been given an honorary degree of D.Litt. by the University of Oxford in 1920, seven years after Cambridge had so honoured him, and he made several visits to both universities in his later years. Another visit he recalls with real feeling, however, was to the great barn on the Kingston Maurward estate, where as a boy he had listened to the village girls singing ballads and dancing to the popular tunes. In *Song to an Old Burden,* he comments sadly:

> **The feet have left the wormholed flooring,**
> **That danced to the ancient air,**
> **The fiddler, all-ignoring,**
> **Sleeps by the gray-grassed 'cello player:**
> **Shall I then foot around around around,**
> **As once I footed there!**

The source of his chief pleasure in old age was the motor car. He had been thrilled enough when the invention of the bicycle gave him the means of going over his beloved countryside at a quicker pace than walking, and now the car introduced him to a new freedom. He was a wealthy man but he did not own a car, merely hired one from a local firm. It was usually an open tourer Mercedes Benz, brought up by the chauffeur to the front door for the old man to get into the bucket seat beside him. Sometimes Florence would be in the back with the picnic basket and they would roam around the scenes of his life and his novels, never at a quicker rate than 25 mph and stopping frequently to gaze at some interesting ruin, or at an old house or inn, or merely at a field of sheep. They went to Marnhull, where his Tess lived as a girl, and to Melbury Osmond where his mother was born, to Bockhampton and the Frome Valley and farther afield to Ilchester and Bath. The old man loved to observe the seasonal changes in the countryside, liked to feel the wind on his face, and noted once after a night drive how he had seen "Orion upside-down in a pool of water under an oak".

Hardy spent his eighty-seventh birthday with friends in Devon, sitting after lunch before a wood fire with a cat on his knee, "staring into the fire", says Florence, "with that deep look of his". He was in a sombre mood when he reached home and she tried to cheer him by telling him of some festivities she was planning for his ninetieth birthday. He told her he intended to spend *that* day in bed: but he was never to reach that great age.

During the autumn of 1927 he was remarkably well and as mentally alert as ever. He and Florence visited their friends as usual, walked a little, went to Stinsford churchyard and scraped the moss off the family tombs, beside which he hoped to be lying one day, spent an hour or two now and then with Kate and Henry, talking of his past life as it unrolled before his inward eye in a series of vivid pictures. Florence reports that he said once that if he had his life to live over again he would prefer to be a small architect in a country town, like John Hicks, and at another time he stated that he had done all he meant to do, but did not know whether it had been worth doing.

His strength began to fail about the middle of December of that year. He felt he could write no more and even his clear, precise handwriting became shaky at last. He did not want to listen to any prose work but he did ask Florence to read Browning's poem *Rabbi Ben Ezra* to him right to the end, on the night of the 10th of January 1928.

On January 11th he seemed brighter and ate grapes and talked with his doctor and some friends. As the light failed, Florence read to him once more, this time a verse from the *Rubáiyát of Omar Khayyám,* then he wanted no more. In the evening he had a heart attack and died about nine o'clock.

In order to please certain people who felt that a Dorset burial was the right thing, Florence consented to have his heart taken from his body so that it could be placed in the grave of his first wife, a strange decision that would surely have been against his wishes. His body in the walnut coffin was wrapped in the red gown of the Cambridge degree and was taken to Woking for cremation, passing on a quiet, grey morning through the villages he had made immortal - Puddletown, Bere Regis, Wimborne and on to Winchester, where Tess's life had ended.

The ashes were interred in Poets' Corner, Westminster Abbey, next to Charles Dickens' tomb and near those of Samuel Johnson, Tennyson and Browning. Florence and Kate were at the ceremony and the pall-bearers were headed by the Prime Minister, who was assisted by writers and poets and the Heads of two colleges of Oxford and Cambridge.

The funeral of the heart at Stinsford was attended by Henry and by a large crowd of local people. Since the church was so small a memorial service took place at the same time in St Peter's Church in Dorchester, and all shops were closed and all business suspended during the time of the service so that Casterbridge could honour its greatest son. In the poem *Afterwards* he had already written his epitaph:

When the Present has latched its postern behind my tremulous stay,
  And the May month flaps its glad green leaves like wings,
Delicate-filmed as new-spun silk, will the neighbours say,
  'He was a man who used to notice such things'?

If it be in the dusk when, like an eyelid's soundless blink,
  The dewfall-hawk comes crossing the shades to alight
Upon the wind-warped upland thorn, a gazer may think,
  'To him this must have been a familiar sight.'

If I pass during some nocturnal blackness, mothy and warm,
  When the hedgehog travels furtively over the lawn,
One may say, 'He strove that such innocent creatures should come to
    no harm,
  But he could do little for them; and now he is gone.'

If, when hearing that I have been stilled at last, they stand at the door,
  Watching the full-starred heavens that winter sees,
Will this thought rise on those who will meet my face no more,
  'He was one who had an eye for such mysteries'?

And will any say when my bell of quittance is heard in the gloom,
  And a crossing breeze cuts a pause in its outrollings,
Till they rise again, as they were a new bell's boom,
  'He hears it not now, but used to notice such things'?

ACKNOWLEDGEMENTS

Acknowledgement is made to the following for kind permission to reproduce photographs:

J R Bennett Esq, Yeovil - Frontispiece and pages 11b, 12a, 20b

Dorset County Library, Thomas Hardy Collection - pages 3, 4, 20a, 26a, 26b, 33

H E F Lock Esq - pages 18a, 18b, 19, 25, 34 - all part of the Lock Collection in Dorset County Library

The Thomas Hardy Society Ltd - Front cover

Trustees of the Thomas Hardy Memorial Collection, Dorset County Museum, Dorchester, Dorset - pages 12b, 17

Dr D G Vulliamy, Bockhampton - page 11a

and to Macmillans, publishers, and Trustees of the Hardy Estate, for permission to quote from the works of Thomas Hardy.